Anthony Rudolf

Absolument présent, dans son visage, Autrui—sans aucune
métaphore—me fait face.
Emmanuel Levinas

Présence de la transparence humaine en son opacité.
Maurice Blanchot

Anthony Rudolf
THE SAME RIVER TWICE

Carcanet New Press
Manchester

To
BRENDA

Some of these poems first appeared in the following publications: *Books Abroad*, *Daedalus Poemcards*, *European Judaism*, *Holy Beggars Gazette*, *Platform*, *The Scotsman*, *Wheels*, *Words Broadsheet*, *Words Etc.*

Five poems are included from *The Manifold Circle* (Carcanet, 1971), an early booklet.

This volume represents what the author wants, at this time, to preserve from poems written between 1964 or 65 and 1976.

First published 1976
by Carcanet New Press Limited
in association with Carcanet Press Limited
330-332 Corn Exchange Buildings
Manchester M4 3BG

Printed in Great Britain
by Eyre & Spottiswoode Limited
at Grosvenor Press, Portsmouth

CONTENTS

AFTER KARL KRAUS

Don't ask what I've been doing all the time.
I hold my tongue;
and I shan't say why.
And there is a stillness when the earth cracks.
No word fitted;
I speak only in my sleep.
And dream of a laughing sun.
It will all pass;
afterwards it makes no difference.
The word passed away, when that world woke up.

ALEXANDRIA, 1930
(a young Jewish poet speaks to old Cavafy)

'You are something of a Jew, Cavafy,
like all poets. Before the crystal night
fragments to stars, will you not walk across
the crooked street to Morpheus, your lover,
who awaits you in his attic, with no pain?
Will your mind not want, upon the midnight,
to flicker with the image of the Lighthouse,
memorial candle shining until the dawn?
Before I take the train to Cairo where
I administer the poor girls' dowry funds,
I beg you, write a poem to Caligula,
a kaddish to the Jews he killed in pogroms
here. This is no city for young men.
I live between your lines. Old man, I love you.'

THE SAME RIVER TWICE

He took my words.
Without a word
He changed the order

Of my things.
Still my poem
Just about.

Much water
Has flowed by.
No word.

But to this day
Ten years on
I write the same

Words. The end
Of all my words
Is a beginning.

'HALF-ASLEEP IN THE TRAIN'

Half-asleep in the train
to old Saint Pancras
he almost sets himself
alight with a cigarette.

Half-awake, he sees,
in the window, someone
swift, nervous, striking him:
it is he, alone,

gesturing, like the twilight
he dared, once, to ignore.

EDWARD HOPPER

Objectivists are metaphysical.
Over against the stillness of the house
what is not still need not be on the move.
And yet, upon my word, the absence moves
to the presence, by the railroad, of the house.
Reality? No way into this house
that is nothing but a structure of his mind
painted alone because it was not there.

THE COTTAGE

Bowing our heads
we enter the room,
see wood beams against
whitewashed stone walls.
The floor is uneven,
fireplace and kettle
unready, unhoused.
Tired, our baby
rattles his toy.
I see in the mirror
him looking through
the window onto
rain and window.

Later we learn
this was the space
of the old labourer
whose forebears had been
tenants for centuries.
In the pub he
tells of the two
inches of ice
over the well
but the horses must still
have their water,
how he often
went to school
without breakfast,
hit over the head
for complaining.

Drinking his sherry
he says his late father
did buy the cottage
from the farmer
but 'I had to sell it
in 1965

because of the threat
of nationalisation.'

I hold my son who
one day will hold
me to my words.
I love this place.
That is the privilege
of the remembrancer.

TRANSLATION

to Evgeny Vinokurov

You are mine host
Please pass me
The bread and the salt

      as it were

Hospitality
To a fault
Is my boast

      as it were

THE EPITAPH OF P(IERRE) M(ENARD)

1 a.m.
Translate I am
into 1.10
a.m.'s English:
I am or *I shall be*.

1 a.m.
Translate I am
into 00.50
a.m.'s English:
I am or *I was*.

1 a.m.
Translate I am
into 1
a.m.'s English:
I am or *I am*.

1: signifier
(here and now)
that I signified
(as it is said)

THE LESSON: A SONNET

A poem is neither a song nor a song of songs.
A poem is neither a mouth nor a tongue.

A poem is not an 'apple'.
A poem is not an apple.

A poem is not a *pomme*.
A poem is not a poemm.

A poem is neither verse nor reverse.
A poem is not a prose is not a prose is not a prose.

A poem is not a serendipity.
A poem is not a machine.

A poem is neither otherness nor liquidity.
A poem is not a Berkeley-quiddity.

Yet
A poem is not nothing but what it is not.

THE REMEMBRANCER/THE SURVIVOR

1.   I said things
that never were,

to reach a new
language was my object.

2.   I write things
that were

to reach an ancient
language I know not.

3.   I shall speak the white night of
the blood of martyrs

and write
the history of silence.

THE COILED NET

The beauty, as
ever, is
describable.
                    Sun
is to *sun*
as a word
goes beneath
another, in pun.

A CAGE WENT IN SEARCH OF A BIRD
Prose for Kafka on the Fiftieth Anniversary of His Death

> 'In His bountiful love for His people Israel, He Himself descended from the Throne of His glory and stood before Moses, until Moses had passed the flames of Sandalfon'
>
> *Legends of the Jews*

> 'If the man is not redeemed in the intervening years, he and his children shall be released in the year of the jubilee'
>
> *Leviticus XXV. 54*

Franz Kafka was hewn from the wall of Jewish Europe.

What have I in common with Jews? I have hardly anything in common with myself and should stand very quietly in a corner, content that I can breathe.

Kafka, absolute writer, purest of writers, lays his head on a pillow of stone.

Yesterday I found the grave. If you look for it timidly it's really almost impossible to find.

As we chant the Kaddish to his name, we say: Prague, dead centre of Europe, dream of Golem, tears of stone.

The commentators' despair.

He is our child. We walk on our roots.

My life is a hesitation before birth.

The stone the builders had doubts about has become the corner-stone.

POTLATCH IN BABEL

Born without a mother tongue, my son
were he inclined in this, that or the other
direction, would not find it difficult
to utter any sound in any language.

(Not) by chance he finds himself between
two speakers of one tongue. Never again
could other languages animadvert
upon his freedom not to recognise
necessity. He imitates, I know,
my imitation of his imitation.

We exchange I for thou, and I put out
my tongue to catch his sounds, and give them back.
Potlatch in Babel is Arcadia.

He smiles: the inter-view is over.
Beneath our dialectic is desire,
unending, for a language of the mother.

AMSTERDAM

Here, late at night, the ground floor window
Is open to the world, and now I under-
stand Vermeer.
                    Even as the girl
Moves about the room she is still life.
Her cat is motionless.
                      I name it Balthus.

Beyond, train after hour moves out
Of this city for another city.

Beside, the canal is filled with works:
A necessary evil gone along with
Before I cross the bridge just as I reach it.

Beside, a house empty of all
It had ever filled;
                      framework without
And oh, the loneliness of surface structures.

Ahead, my hotel room where memories
Are framed; aided, abetted by the text.

Here, by the ground floor window is
A mirror, where the girl may see the world
And not be seen seeing, in the eyes
Of me, who know she sees.
                        Dutch life
Reveals art: is text; Vermeer draws Balthus.

KAFKA'S TOMB

*'Yesterday I found the grave. If you look for it
timidly it's really almost impossible to find.'*
—Kafka

I ask my friend to visit Kafka's grave.
She finds the cemetery.
She climbs the fence.
Impossible to identify the tomb,
like an unnumbered room
in the corridor of an insurance office.

The undergrowth is overgrown.
In bad Czech she asks two boys
which is Kafka's grave.
They smile; they flap their arms.
Kafka is a jackdaw,
a jackdaw with a human face.

The wounded jackdaw is
no match
for the fire.

BALTHUS

1.

His virgins meditate, they stare into
the space of time, dream in the light of day.

Said (wrongly) to be 'the painter', his cats
sit around the colour, at a stroke.

I look upon the dream of his Thérèse
(the cat sups milk), whose thighs are open to

'the world': at last I understand that if
we are not—and we are not—*voyeurs*

then we are Thérèse. I catch the eye
of the girl beside me. I am Thérèse,

innocent, pure and exiled adolescent
dreaming exile, purity and innocence.

2.

He draws the light, the sting of memory.
Repose accuses, stillness calls. The silence

of a Balthus virgin screams across
the centuries to Piero and Mantegna.

She whispers, whispers to herself that no
action shall be sister to the dream.

CHAGALL MUSEUM, NICE

The graven images elucidate,
their lustre
a cycle
of tellings,
arching
over the horizon
of my remembrance, to the vault
of childhood, the unlocked
stronghold:

stories, sight unseen, made their
entrance
in my head
then and there,

and now his views
and my re-
views
conjoin, unite, marry
beneath the canopy, the covenant,
of generations:

Jacob and the angel
clarified
in the burning bush of memory;

we leave,
like Adam and Eve,
this artificial paradise, it
is in the nature
of things,
like a ladder
or like a rock that water
is struck
from.

CHEZ MAEGHT

Before the entrance is the fore-play,
pleasure-garden of the lovely
museum: I look, I am entranced.
The text restores attention to
a metamorphosis, the way
all reflection doubles back
upon itself, a mirror-image
and my strategic pose seen through.
I listen hard—the metalanguage
of stone is under-
      stood by grass:
such elemental purity!,
such inter-diction, fatal lack
of flaw in evidence. I pass
by the Calder mobile danced
by the wind. Before the pond
and the geometries beyond
sits a dog as immobile
and silent as a Balthus cat.
I go in. To the Balthus. Smile.
The little tiger smells a rat.

SAINT-PAUL DE VENCE

Once more I name
                    a city where the stone
inspired a life, a life inspired the stone.
It was a place whose 'moral shape . . . and moulds
of commonwealth' revealed themselves within
its walls of refuge, where a life was lived,
not happiness pursued, though happy you
died, assured of continuity.

Now it is thanks to commerce that the old
place survives, and thanks to commerce will
die tomorrow. Why complain of that,
since this reprieve is after-life? The ancient
city yields the time before a poem.

Our house is always open to the sun
beating on a wall where, like my hand,
a lizard flees. I say: we are the sign
the place was here. My pregnant wife sleeps on.

KENSINGTON PALACE GARDENS

I walk across the park,
Across the day, humid, foreign,
To the orangery.

The merest
Hint of breeze, of rain
Announces
Perfection or a mood I thought
Dead for ever, like a dead
Woman, or something uttered in vain.

Inside the orangery:
No hint of breeze, of rain,

Announces
Perfection or a mood I used to think
Dead for ever, like a dead
Woman, or something

Uttered in the merest
Hint of breeze, of rain
As I walk back
Across the park,
Across the day, humid, foreign.

DISJUNCT

To spend
a few days in the house of our friends.

To listen
to their music, to their absence.

To read
the bits and pieces,
back numbers
of magazines we do not take.

To answer
the phone that would have gone unanswered.

Here, all is dis-
junct as if my spectacles were lost.

THE TELLING, THE FOURFOLD DEATH

I sought my poems in the city.
I could not find them.
Then I did remember where
I had left them.
          I returned
and they were still there,
more or less was the pity.

    *

At the burning of the books
the paper turned to ash
but the letters wept,
like God when Israel sins,
and floated up to heaven,
brighter than any star.

    *

Died this week the last immortal.
No choice but to seek another.

The child: immortal is the child,
too young to know I am not mortal.

    *

Had Rimbaud died in the Commune
we would not know his name.

Others died, nameless
and in vain, unless

we live, write against
their absence.

To read again
the book I loved.
No,
to read again
the book I loved
at a time when
I did this or that.
The book may be
the same, what is not
is the relation
between us:
that old dialectic
(fifth horseman) rides
roughshod over
the bones of our dead
whom we envy.

In his death
they let him down

slowly, carefully
into the grave

and all shovel earth
over him

to share the blame
as it is said

In his life
they let him down

THE CRUNCH

Beside me on the train a girl
with a kitten, the kitten eyes
the mountain; mountain: the first
snows of this year. I divide
attention between my
book and a low stone wall.

Suddenly two horses
run towards the North.
Suddenly I know I
have to write; resist:

No:
        in Scotland my head
comes together in these words,
for the time of a poem I marry
the *Shekhina*: I redeem her
from exile: we are two horses
running towards the North.

PAIR

The door rattles.
The wind blows.
The clock ticks.

The time is still.
The
We pass by

Hurrying slowly
Together, two
Is an odd number

Vasko Popa said just write
(as the American poets do)
what happened to you one day.
O.K. Vasko, here goes: we went
to a poetry reading where
we did not understand a word
and I thought to write this poem.
What else happened today? We talked,
or was it last night, of Petru's friends
in Bucharest, the body-washers.
Better stay alive! We ex-
changed proverbs. You told me about
your interest in wolves and
you said this, and I said that.
Of course, you understand, Vasko,
one can write like this all night.

Vasko Popa, emperor-priest,
I shall ride away tomorrow
up on one of your yo-yo-
cycles, and howl with the wolves.

THE BEARS OF SARAJEVO

In the old city of Dubrovnik
even reconstructed sites are beautiful.
Only pedestrians are allowed within the walls.
We wander and wander the narrowest streets.
Here is the synagogue, locked this night.
Here an American student is singing
and here we find a simple restaurant.

At dinner I talk Russian with a man
from Sarajevo: he tells me a Turkish proverb:
only bears and Christians want to live in
his town in winter when it rains like England.
Now it is time to go to the concert
in the Dominican church: Rossini Mass;
and lemon tea before we catch the bus.

So we have been in the old city
of Dubrovnik, wandered its narrowest streets.
It might have been Safed or Colchester
but it was the one and only
old city of Dubrovnik, once Rapallo.
Old city. Cherish. Old. Sad joy:
made to man's measure, a perfect fit.

DUBROVNIK POEM (EMILIO TOLENTINO)

'The Jew was always treated
well, in this part of the world.
Zudioska Ulica,
this street, the Jews have lived in
always. You see the grilles?
Behind them the women sat,
entering the dark space
by way of our house next door.
My family has cared for
the synagogue from there
for rather more than three
hundred years. The little
gallery was built later.'

'Now we are seventeen,
seven men in all Dubrovnik,
not even a *minyan*. Six
hundred years it has stood,
this synagogue, on this street.
And I am old. I am ill.'

'Always the Jew was treated
well, in this part of the world.
From Venice we came, from Spain.
When we came back from Auschwitz
the archives had disappeared:
plundered, lost, destroyed,
gone, like so many lives.
Hidden under floorboards
some we retrieved, some treasures.'

'Solomon Tolentino,
my ancestor, signed in Hebrew
that scrap of paper pasted
up on the wall downstairs;
dead in the sixteen-hundred
and-sixty-seven earthquake.

The synagogue survived it.
This letter came from Moses
Montefiore with thanks
for our congratulations
sent on his hundredth birthday.'

'AFTER THE DREAM'

After the dream,
after no sleep
I entered the room.

I put on the fire.
Half-light inside,
outside half-light
speak to each other.

The whole light
touches my darkness.
All is window.
All is shadow.

It is beyond me.
Tomorrow
I shall not journey.

I see the college entrance through my window.
If I were you, would you be me?,
                    asked Michael,
sleep on the problem.
               No; were Michael me,
why then, perhaps, I'd be free to become
the real thing, object, stone.
                  You know, what
I tend to write about: let vehicle
be tenor.
        But when Michael *is* Michael
why am I not me? Why is the country
of the self torn from the back-country
of the self, is the question I do ask
myself.

THE VISIT

You know when they know they are dying before
            their time.
·They say goodbye.
The very old need never say goodbye:
their very presence emblem of farewell.

Her brother is buried in Warsaw.
She went to see the tomb.
Even believers say goodbye
to a dead man and his living wife.

THE FIRE

Three in the morning, I leave our bed
because of the pain in my foot.
Swollen, it wants swinging around
like a baby, to forget whatever
is troubling it: today I fell down
a stair as I rushed to the door
to let in the engineer. My god,
three days without a phone, and now
another limb wrecked. I go
into the lounge. The fire. Uneasily
as I read and easily the moment
I put down the book I remember
my fear: that in my absence the fire
will burn down my house. Time after
time after time I check the fire
is off. Always it is. What if
I were the first person I know
to lose all in a fire? Ah
it would be that clearing of debts
I have always promised myself
as a prelude to writing *the* poem.
My notes would be dropped in the dustbin,
my books, my books would litter the floor,
my nostalgia at last be consumed
in the fire of presence. The fire.

SONG

I loved the man,
I loved the book.

I quarrelled
with the man, as the man
quarrels with his own book, always.

Now
I quarrel with the book
twice over.

HUMPTY DUMPTY

The crack two-thirds the way
down our mirror disjoins
the reflection.
                    My reflexion
is like that. I disjoin
my images. Only I'd
put them together again.

THE VOICE, THE STILLNESS

Near Puddle Dock, remembered wasteland
of The Mermaid; near my old school;
by the Church of Saint Magnus Martyr:
that stillness of Saint Mary at Hill,

that peace no synagogue yields me;
that silence, like sexual innocence,
the voice of a Jewess will tear.
The vicar prays for the musicians.

Timeless, music. No, it has its own
good time quotidian time yearns for.
The song of this woman returns us
to York's Eden before the expulsion.

This place a great fire consumed
three centuries ago, once again
is consumed by a passion: the voice
of Jerusalem, City of Peace.

Drills plough through chartered streets outside:
redeemers of the land live on.
Of old London Bridge, nothing
remains but an arch on dry land.

Sways a row
of trees darkly,
silently,
through a field
of black velvet.
At right angles
flash the lights
of occasional
heavy lorries,
the same lorries,
it may be,
that woke me
in the South.

Now I hold
to one axis,
now I hold
to the other.
And now, for a brief
moment, an edge
of light catches
the trees: light
and trees are
pulled, like lovers,
like words, together,
two modalities
yielding perfection?

ENGLAND

Down Grey Street, and Dean Street
past Dog Leap Stairs
to the house of Bessy Surtees
by the Tyne River.
Here, Bessy eloped
with the future Lord Chancellor
in 1772. We go up
to the first floor,
inspect the window.
By the one she left from
is a bull's eye pane.
We look at the same river twice.
Then through the house
and out the back door,
along and up
winding steps to a point
before the Lawcourts, and look
back on the house,
all timber and timber,
landscape I cherish.
Wood is for memory,
lined like an old man,
stained with the presence
of Bessy and unnamed
people I name here.
The top-floor tenants
walk a heritage. I wag
the tail of their cat
as I enter the frame.
We leave. It decomposes.
From the Lawcourts, the bridge
a Puritan conscience and
commerce meet half way on.

ABSENCE

A friend, long absent, calls me up.
We talk of mutual friends,
lost, stolen, strayed.
                    We link
circuits we've been absent from.

Separated lives meet for an instant.
How is . . . ? Have you seen . . . ?
Is she still . . . ? Does he live . . . ?
I wait for an answer.
                    If they

are nothing now I was nothing then.
Outside, the sound of rain is falling
coloured by a night Sunday.
Across the road: a gathering

in the ground floor apartment.
Laughter.
            My wife is asleep.

LATE NIGHT MOVIE

The cathode swallows Cagney like a whirlpool.
A cat squalls in the back end of the garden.

Once I ran a dog down near Saint-Malo
in the middle of a night without my lover.

This humid night bears down like a silent rapist.
My wife sleeps beneath an appalling white sheet.

I cut up the lines of some beautiful poems
as if they are limbs in a terrible experiment.

Ann Arbor's Arboretum is surely not peaceful
and down the road motel beds vibrate for a quarter.

Something is between my shadow and my voice.

THE STRUCTURE

I am going home. The smoke
across the bridge
mimes the waves of thought

driving
alone
yields.

I shall remember
where I have been, and my smile
frozen to the bridge

The foot of the bed
now faced the door.

My mother told me
what it signified.

Wanting to remain
alive, I moved the bed

and just to be
on the safe side

became the unbeliever
I always believed I was.

COLLECTED POEM

It is time I published my collected places.
They have been gathering dust
in old files, in a cupboard, in my study
and I am ready to bring them together.

I shall not collect the ones passed through
so rapidly I put no roots down,
as in a bad poem or one-night stand.
They happened: that is already something.

I open a file to the elements
of remembered memories, as once
by the lake in Chicago I remembered
a walk, I buried, along the Cambridge Backs.

THE HOUSE OF EMPTINESS

'That sad picture? Many years ago
I lusted after it. A few years later
the friend who drew it, and her husband,
gave it to me as a wedding present.

'A presence tinges my remembering—
not of some event, but that good time's
structure, open-ended, of infinite
dispositions and possibilities, I thought.

'It is a house of emptiness, a house
of no gesture, and no flickering
recognition lightens the stillness
within those trees, that fence before the trees,

'within the field drawn as another fence:
all is stasis beyond the fated stasis
of the charcoal images of death in life;
the image of unspoken absence speaks.'

TO THE ONION'S HEART

Must do this,
and that
before I write.
Oh, the excellence of my excuses
for not writing the book
that will negate
all other books.
Too tired;
so much to do:
a living to be earned,
things to translate,
to read,
letters to type,
people to see,
family to cherish.

One by one
I strip away the layers.
All commitments honoured,
what is there to do
but write that book *à la Blanchot*?
What do I do?
I write poems
even I know
are the ultimate excuse,
the last word in beginnings.
The eye of the storm is closed.

CHECKPOINT CHARLIE

I put my book on the table,
stretch myself.
I am tired.
The time has come again
for wandering around the room
before I am allowed to go to bed.
I switch the record-player off,
pull out the plug
and push the point-switch up.
Then I tidy my desk
and I tidy it again,
again,
and just before I leave the room
I wander over
to the record-player
and check the point again.
I switch off the light,
and leave the room,
and close the door.
And open the door again,
make sure the light's out,
peer beneath the shade
and eye the bulb.
I go back to the door,
switch on the light,
so that I know for sure what's on,
what's off,
then turn out the light again.
And leave the room,
and close the door.
And open the door again.
Admit the fucking light is off,
suppose it's safe
to go to bed at last.

THE ROSE, THE LAND
(Paul Celan, 1920-1970)

It was evening of the rose
and you fled
(as crows
fly) the unbecoming dead
across
the field of presence,
that sea of frozen violence,
whose atroc-
ities
of thorn demand
no return to ancient cities,
to the blue land
on the other side
of being, en-
closed. After you died
did ten
sing you to eternal rest
of life, to your rebirth
and fill your grave with song of common earth
as you laid your head on Shulamith's breast?

THE WANDERER

Where is home for the ray of nervous
energy slanting to the air
who lives in the City of Peace and whose
loner's body fills so little space
if not *here and now*, in every place?

His God is dead and symbols lack
all meaning, so drinking from rocks,
splitting the wind, he sings the real,
celebrates the harvest with friends
in a vanished city sought through sand.

This *chassid* dances, whose heaven is
quotidian earth where *is* is sacred:
in his language wine and bread
are only *once* removed from the real,
are twice holy for that. The language
is remembrance. He sings an ancient
song of the earth; his dance is ancient
as his village, resists all absence.

PEBBLE

Pebble: 'magic mountain', packed
tight with sediment, with veins
through oceans of a long night.

Pebble: core of rock-pool, wind
and rain the sand consumes, chock-
a-block like a diamond, a scream.

Pebble: an energy at one
with being alone, with absence
of artefact, with failings of men.

THE MANIFOLD CIRCLE

Apparent perfection is
my undoing.

With no line to follow
that does not swallow
itself,

my heads go round in
circles, overlap: the only

way into one
is across another.

I try to stay
around the first one—
is the devil I know;

then what, I try
to leave it all to itself

but I is not the one

and the same old thing.

One more week, one less week:
a century of hands shall not cover
this day, evil, timeless, alone,
with no home of week, and empty
of hours, all time minute, untold.

I am going round my
head is going round
me all around me.

Vertigo is a white
absence half-way home.

THROUGH THE WINDOW

You are late tonight, maybe you won't come.
I hang suspended, or I walk night's
waters, then you appear, a whiteness
like breath in cold air on winter mornings.
Out there we merge each other on our life's
other side, and we are two in one,
in little death forget contingence and
strike out along a tangent of oblivion,
serene as stone. I turn, face the room.
You are late tonight, maybe you won't come.

THE HYACINTH

The bird has its own
reasons for singing
and I have no mind,
no heart to say so.

I seek inter-
pretation: the bird
suggests the pure
notes in darkness

sung by a distant
voice from a window,
the music drifting
over strangely

as I walk early
one night, and try
not to be one
with all about me

and even if
the hyacinth
did not speak of
Sappho, I'd still

fail for reasons
I am hard put
to ignore. The bird
has stopped singing.

THE GRAVE

Weather-beaten;
weeds and earth
erase the words.

Time lowers
itself slowly
but surely a death
was lived
that the stone be
thus / the past:
palpable, eroded.

Here and there
I make out
letters,
even words.

The dust within
the tomb is closer
to the stone
than I am. Now
place is sign.

TOUCH STONES

I disturb them, to be reassured
nothing is beyond me.
They are deeply touched, their night's
sleep is not distressed
by that recognition.

I would embrace them, see through them,
learn of ashes behind the wall
that I ought to know already.
The wall must be gone through. I must
burn my fingers in the ashes.

NOTES

p. 11   *Edward Hopper.* American painter, 1882-1967.

p. 14   *Translation.* The Russian word for 'hospitality', translated word-for-word, is 'bread-and-salt'.

p. 15   *Pierre Menard.* A character in an early story of Borges that can be read as a parable of translation.

p. 19   *A Cage Went in Search of a Bird.* The passages in italics are quotes from Kafka.

p. 21   *Amsterdam* (see also p. 23, *Balthus*, and p. 25, *Chez Maeght*). Balthus: contemporary French painter.

p. 22   *Kafka's Tomb.* Later it turned out to be the wrong cemetery. The word *Kafka* is Czech for *jackdaw*.

p. 24   *Chagall Museum, Nice.* The last stanza alludes to an aspect of Pound's poetics.

p. 26   *Saint-Paul de Vence.* The words quoted are from an early poem by Donald Davie.

p. 30   *'Tout lecteur est l'élu d'un livre'.* This quotation is taken from Edmond Jabès's most recent book *Le livre des ressemblances* (Gallimard, 1976).

p. 32   *The Crunch.* 'The Shekhina' in Judaism is God's Divine Presence. It is the only name of God which is of the feminine gender. For Jewish mystics, it is the female aspect of God.

p. 36   *Dubrovnik Poem.* Minyan is a Hebrew word with the meaning of 'quorum'. Ten male worshippers over the age of thirteen comprise a quorum for congregational purposes. (See also p. 55, *The Rose, the Land*.)

p. 44   *The Voice, the Stillness.* York: in 1190 the Jews of York killed themselves rather than surrender to the incited mob. Expulsion: in 1290 Edward I expelled the Jews from England.

p. 53   *To the Onion's Heart.* Blanchot: French writer, born 1907.